Hands-On Science

MOTION

Lola M. Schaefer ✳ *Illustrated by Druscilla Santiago*

᛫ᚿᚾᛁ Charlesbridge

Welcome to the physics lab!

Here you can have fun exploring forces—
what they are and what they do.
Feel free to push, pull, poke, tap, and
slide any objects on display.

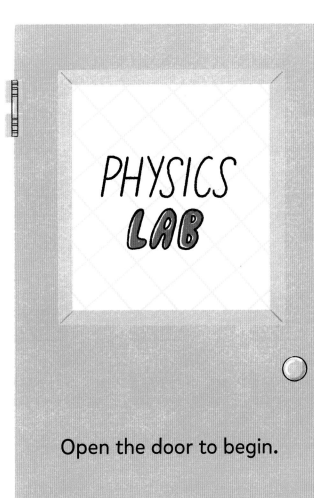

PHYSICS LAB

Open the door to begin.

This whipped cream is at rest.

Give it a poke.
Go ahead.

The whipped cream looks different.
The **force** of your finger moved
the cream and changed its shape.

A force is a push or pull that can change
the motion or shape of an object.
You can't see forces,
but you can see what they do.

Turn this book upside down
and shake it.

Uh-oh!

Most of the whipped cream fell.
Gravity pulled the cream
off the page and onto the floor.
Gravity is a force that pulls objects
toward Earth.

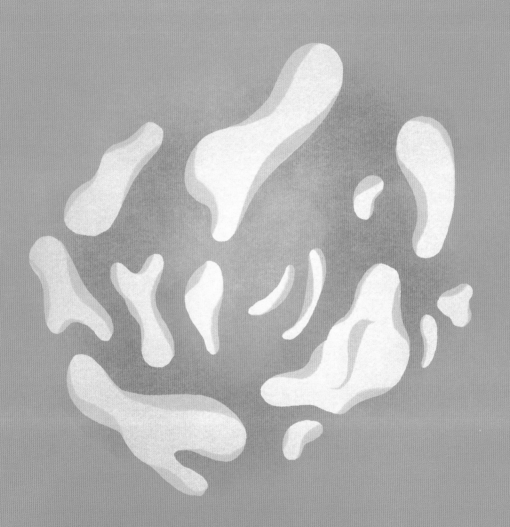

Turn the page to see more!

This track is level.

The marble is at rest.

But not for long.

Tilt the book to the right—
just a little.

Whoosh!

Gravity pulls the marble down
the track until . . .

Bonk!

The block pushes against
the marble and stops it.
An object in motion tends to
remain in motion unless
acted upon by another force.

Slowly tilt the book to the left.
Stop when the track is level.

The marble is again at rest.

This time, tilt the book
even further to the right.
Angle the track down,
down, down toward the floor.

Zoom!

The marble accelerates, rolling
down the track faster and faster.
The steeper the incline,
the faster an object moves.

Quick!

Push the block out of the way.

Where did the marble go?

It rolled right out of
the book. Gravity pulled
it to the floor.

Turn the page for
a different experiment.

Here are two beanbags.

One is on ice.

The other is on sandpaper.

Tilt the book downward toward your toes.
Just a bit.

Oops! Gravity pulled the beanbags toward Earth. The beanbag on the ice slid off the page. The other beanbag slid, but only a little.

The **friction** between the beanbag and the rough sandpaper slowed the beanbag. Friction is a force that happens when two objects rub against each other.

What else can create force? How about water or wind?

Here's a small mound of dirt
and an eyedropper filled with water.

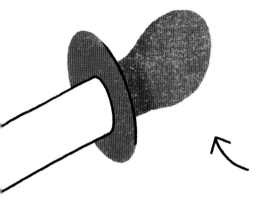

Squeeze the end of the eyedropper three times.

1... 2... 3...

Look!

Those three drops of water pushed
some of the dirt up and out.

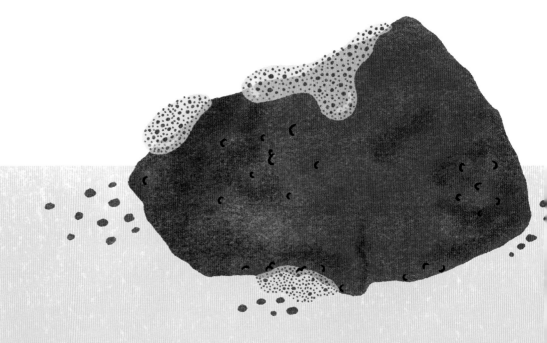

Imagine what more water can do.

Think of the force of a river or an ocean wave!

Wind can create force, too.

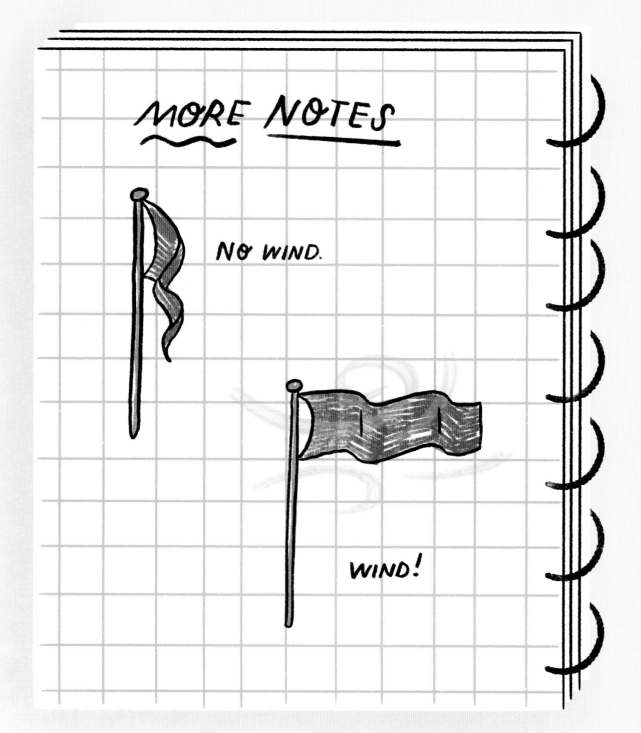

Put your lips close to this pile of sand.
Shut your eyes and blow—blow hard.

Sand flew everywhere!
What a mess!

Press the button
to start the Lab-Vac.

Vrooom. Vrooom.

Inside the Lab-Vac, a fan spins
and pulls some of the air out
of the hose. This creates a vacuum.
Anything that gets near the hose
is sucked inside.

PHYSICS LAB

All clean!

Turn the page to open
the door and leave the lab.

As you go about your day,
look all around.

Can you see forces at work?
Are they pushes or pulls?
Gentle or strong?
How can you tell?

Push, Pull, Go!

You create forces every moment of every day.

At the park, you push a ball.
It speeds down, hits the ground,
and bounces back up.

In the classroom, you pull a door,
and it swings open.

In the kitchen, you push a bowl sideways.
It slides across the table.

In your bedroom, you pull a cord,
and it moves your blinds.

In the garage, you pull a handle,
and the garage door rolls open.

 What other forces do you make
that move objects up, down,
in, or out?

Teeter-Totter Down, Up, and Away

Always experiment with a grown-up.

MATERIALS

- Drinking straw
- Craft stick
- Ruler
- Pencil
- Small object such as an action figure, a cotton ball, or a spool of thread

PROCEDURE

1. Measure the craft stick and mark the middle with a pencil.

2. Place the middle of the craft stick across the straw to form a teeter-totter.

3. Place your small object on one end of the craft stick. What happens?

4. Gently tap the other end of the craft stick. What happens? If the object fell off, put it back on.

5. This time, slap the end of the craft stick—hard!

When you put the object on one end of the teeter-totter, the force of gravity pulled the object and that end down. When you tapped or slapped the teeter-totter, your hand created a force that pushed the stick and made it move. The more force you applied, the greater the movement.

For Octavia—L. M. S.

For my mom, who keeps me going—D. S.

Special thanks to Dr. R. Bruce Ward, retired astronomy educator, Center for Astrophysics | Harvard & Smithsonian, for sharing his invaluable expertise and advice.

Published by Charlesbridge
9 Galen Street, Watertown, MA 02472
(617) 926-0329
www.charlesbridge.com

Library of Congress Cataloging-in-Publication Data
Names: Schaefer, Lola M., 1950– author. | Santiago, Druscilla, illustrator.
Title: Motion / Lola M. Schaefer; illustrated by Druscilla Santiago.
Description: Watertown, MA: Charlesbridge, [2024] | Series: Hands-on science | Audience: Ages 4–8 |
Audience: Grades 2–3 | Summary: "In this interactive picture book, young readers poke, roll,
and slide objects on the page, using their imagination to conduct simple physics experiments.
They learn about forces (pushes and pulls), inertia, gravity, acceleration, and friction. Back matter
includes a real-world experiment."–Provided by publisher.
Identifiers: LCCN 2022058424 (print) | LCCN 2022058425 (ebook) |
ISBN 9781623542450 (hardcover) | ISBN 9781632897121 (ebook)
Subjects: LCSH: Motion–Juvenile literature.
Classification: LCC QC127.4 .S327 2024 (print) | LCC QC127.4 (ebook) |
DDC 531/.11–dc23/eng/20230608
LC record available at https://lccn.loc.gov/2022058424
LC ebook record available at https://lccn.loc.gov/2022058425

Printed in China
(hc) 10 9 8 7 6 5 4 3 2 1

Illustrations done in digital media
Text type set in Mikado by Hannes von Doehren
Printed by 1010 Printing International Limited in Huizhou, Guangdong, China
Production supervision by Jennifer Most Delaney
Designed by Cathleen Schaad